Adventure with Alphabet

The A to Z of Fruits

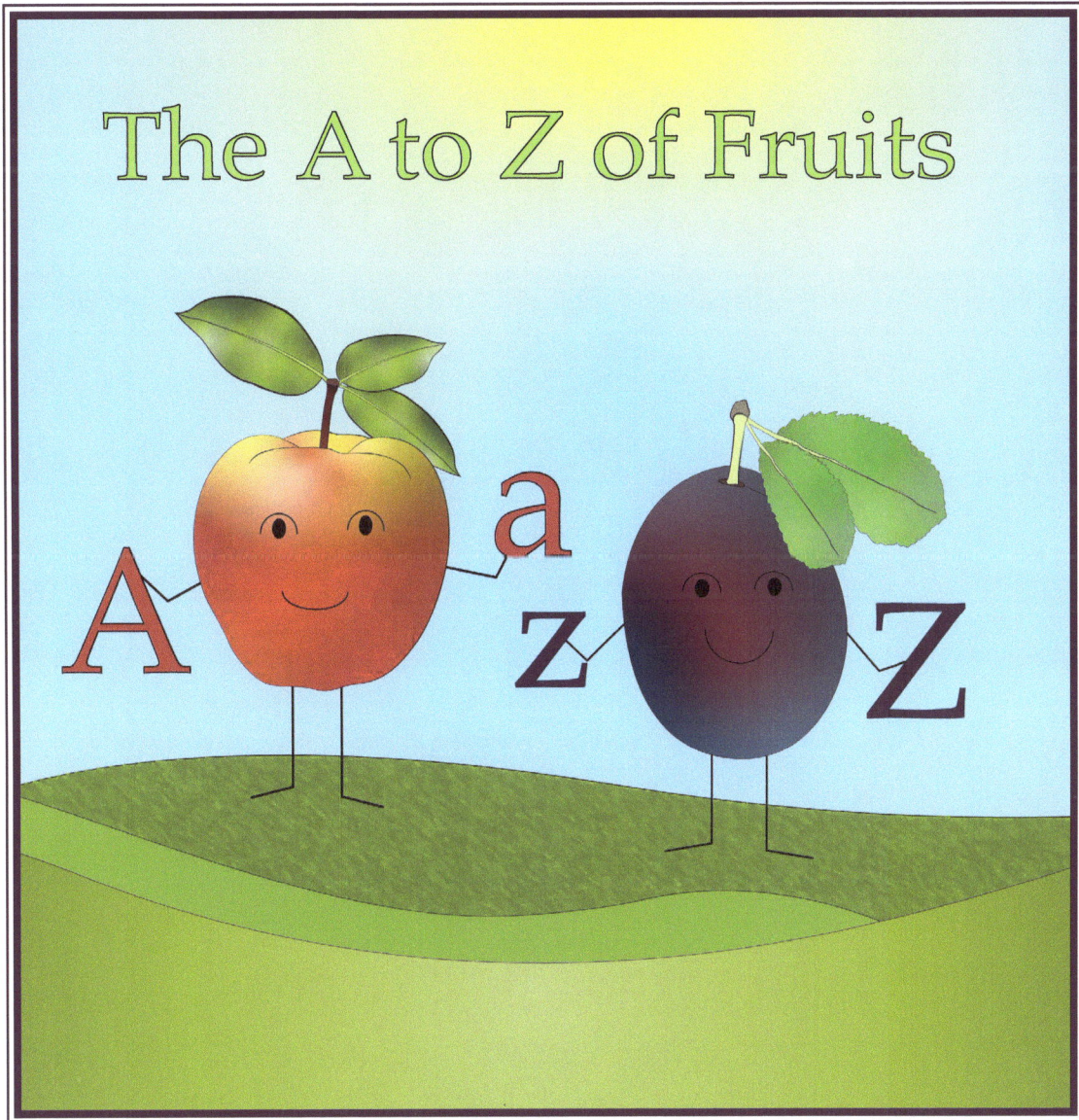

Written, Art & Design
by
Katarzyna Skrzyniecka & Mateusz Skrzyniecki

ISBN 979-8-88713-012-5
Library of Congress Control Number 2025905146

www.adventurewithalphabet.com

Adventure with Alphabet
The A to Z of Fruits

THIS BOOK BELONGS TO

Aa Bb Cc Dd
Ee Ff Gg Hh Ii
Jj Kk Ll Mm
Nn Oo Pp Qq
Rr Ss Tt Uu Vv
Ww Xx Yy Zz

Curious Explorers!

Get ready for a delicious and colorful journey through the alphabet!

From A to Z, each letter introduces a special fruit,
bringing the world of nature to life in a fun and exciting way.

You'll meet some familiar favorites like
Blueberry, Strawberry, and Watermelon,
but you'll also discover unique fruits from around the world—
have you ever heard of Ugni, Ximenia Caffra or Zwetschge?

With each turn of the page, you'll explore new flavors, shapes,
and names while learning the alphabet one fruit at a time.

This book is a great way to build your knowledge, spark curiosity,
and celebrate the beauty of nature's bounty.

Whether you're reading alone or sharing with friends and family,
every page is a chance to learn something new.

So, let's begin our Alphabet Adventure—
what fruity surprises will we find?

— Kasia & Mati

My English name is

Apple

My German name is Apfel.

Aa

My English name is

Blueberry

My Czech name is Borůvka.

Bb

My English name is
Cherry
My French name is Cerise.

C c

My English name is

Dewberry

My Dutch name is Dauwbes.

Dd

My English name is
Elderberry
My Hungarian name is Bodza.

Ee

My English name is

Forest Strawberry

My Polish name is Poziomka.

Ff

My English name is

Grape

My Spanish name is Uva.

G g

My English name is

Honeydew

My Czech name is Medový Meloun.

Hh

My English name is
Indian Gooseberry
My Dutch name is Indiase kruisbes.

Ii

My English name is
Jostaberry

My German name is Jostabeere.

J j

My English name is
Kiwi
My Polish name is Kiwi.

My English name is

Lemon

My Italian name is Limone.

L l

My English name is
Manzano Banana
My Hungarian name is Manzano Banán.

M m

My English name is
Nectarine
My French name is Nectarines.

My English name is

Orange

My Czech name is Pomeranč.

O o

My English name is

Pineapple

My Spanish name is Piña.

P p

My English name is

Quince

My Dutch name is Kweeper.

Qq

My English name is

Raspberry

My Polish name is Malina.

Rr

My English name is

Strawberry

My Italian name is Fragola.

Ss

My English name is
Taylor Gold Pear
My Spanish name is Pera Taylor Gold.

Tt

My English name is

Ugni

My Hungarian name is Chilei Mirtuszfa.

U u

My English name is

Van Dyke Mango

My French name is Mangue Van Dyke.

V v

My English name is

Watermelon

My German name is Wassermelone.

Ww

My Botanical - English name is

Ximenia Caffra - Sour Plum

My Spanish name is Ciruela Agria.

Xx

My English name is

Yellow Dragon Fruit

My Italian name is Frutto del Drago Giallo.

Yy

My German name is
Zwetschge
My English name is Damson Plum.

Zz

Congratulations, Curious Explorers!

You've traveled from A to Z,
discovering fruits from near and far—
tasting the alphabet, learning names,
and seeing how special each fruit is!

Now that you've met all these colorful characters,
you might spot them at the market, in your lunchbox,
or even growing in a garden or orchard nearby.

Remember, every fruit has its own story, flavor,
and secret to share— just like you!
Keep asking questions, trying new things,
and celebrating the wonders of the natural world.

Our fruity adventure may be over for now,
but your curiosity can keep growing every day.

Until our next tasty tale…

Stay sweet, stay curious,
Kasia & Mati

www.ingramcontent.com/pod-product-compliance
Lightning Source LLC
LaVergne TN
LVHW072056070426
835508LV00002B/119